Marketing

101

Business Reading for Schoolgoers

Rhea Mehta

Marketing 101 : Essential Business Knowledge for Schoolgoers

Rhea Mehta assisted by Siddharth Mehta

First Edition

Marketing is a contest for people's attention

Dedicated to all those children, as they pass through the stage that I am currently passing through: Exploring what I want to be!

Contents

Chapters

Author's Foreword

Hello Everyone.

Enter Class X and people all around you start asking "What do you plan to do when you grow up? What subjects do you want to take?" These are tough questions for a fifteen year old but people expect crisp and ready answers. I realized, it's not only the inquisitiveness of people that you need to satisfy but you do need to have these answers for your own self so that you are able to make up your mind and start focusing your energies in the direction that you would like to build your career in.

I was fortunate to do a two week summer internship in an advertising company followed by an on-line course in Marketing from Coursera which tickled my interest in the subject. I understood that marketing is an integral part of all our lives as all of us at all times are transacting goods, services, experiences or relationships with each other. In order for these transactions to happen the other party must see value in them. The art and science of creating, demonstrating and communicating value is what marketing is all about. I have therefore decided to pursue Marketing as a career.

The purpose of this book is to give a glimpse and a basic understanding of what marketing is to all high school students, so that they can consider it as one of their career choices. Besides, since marketing is anyway so intrinsically intertwined in our lives, an appreciation of the subject would anyway help you in whatever career you may finally choose to take.

I hope you like it.

Introduction

Let me tell you a story.

There is a maternity home in Delhi where more than a dozen children are born everyday and since most of them need special care they are kept in a nursery for the first few days. So if you go into the nursery at any time you hear a cacophony with all the babies crying; wanting to be lifted and cuddled. The nurses are invariably indifferent to these babies as it is commonplace for them to see the babies crying at all times.

There was a smart new born. He hated the nursery and instead wanted to be lifted, cuddled and taken out of this horrible place. But how does he let his intentions be known; nobody paid any heed to what he thought or wanted.

He probably had some pre-natal lessons in marketing and therefore decided that instead of crying, he should smile each time the nurse was passing by. He differentiated himself from the other cranky babies and communicated this through his smile to the nurse.

This caught the nurse's attention and since everyone likes happy and smiling babies and, wants to indulge with them, the nurse picked him up in her arms, cuddled him and played with him.

He was thus out of his misery. That's what marketing can do!

We often hear and use the term 'Marketing' glibly, without understanding the profound implications and consequences it has on our day-to-day life.

Any good company uses a multitude of legitimate means to increase its profit and to promote its business - *Marketing* is one of them. The marketing strategies and tactics used by companies act as a stimulus, which instigate in the client the desire to purchase a particular good or service.

The strength of good marketing is immense. It is the reason why a company producing identical goods and services as others, may distinguish itself from its competition and achieve success. For instance when we think of the phrase "social media", Facebook comes to our mind immediately. This leads to the question, why did Orkut or Hi5 or Myspace not come to our mind or why did they fail?

In this book, my aim is to dwell on the reasons why these certain names pop up in our mind or why we prefer to buy products or services from certain companies and not others. And why often companies with superior goods are left out while others gain a large market share.

Importance of Marketing

Theoretically, marketing is defined as the process of establishing and communicating the value of a product or service to customers thereby convincing them to buy the same. To many of us, the moment we hear of marketing, images of flashy sales people trying to sell us a useless product or TV Ads showing a famous Bollywood or Hollywood actress endorsing a product or internet banners goading us to click on the 'buy now' button or chasing us from one website to another, come to mind. Yes, marketing includes all that and much more.

It starts with understanding your product or service, who are the likely customers for that product or service, what need of the customers does your product or service satisfy, who else in the industry is trying to address similar needs through similar products, how will you differentiate yourself from others, how will you communicate the value that you provide to your potential customers and finally how will you push or encourage your potential customers to actually buy the product or service? Marketing encompasses all this.

Human Needs

The subject of marketing can be approached from different viewpoints and explained variously but first let me try and explain the needs of a man as they evolve with his economic and social progress because the whole idea of selling any products or services is to satisfy a buyer's needs. These needs have been best described by Abraham Maslow's 'Hierarchy of Needs' which is also popularly known as the 'Theory of Self Actualization' :

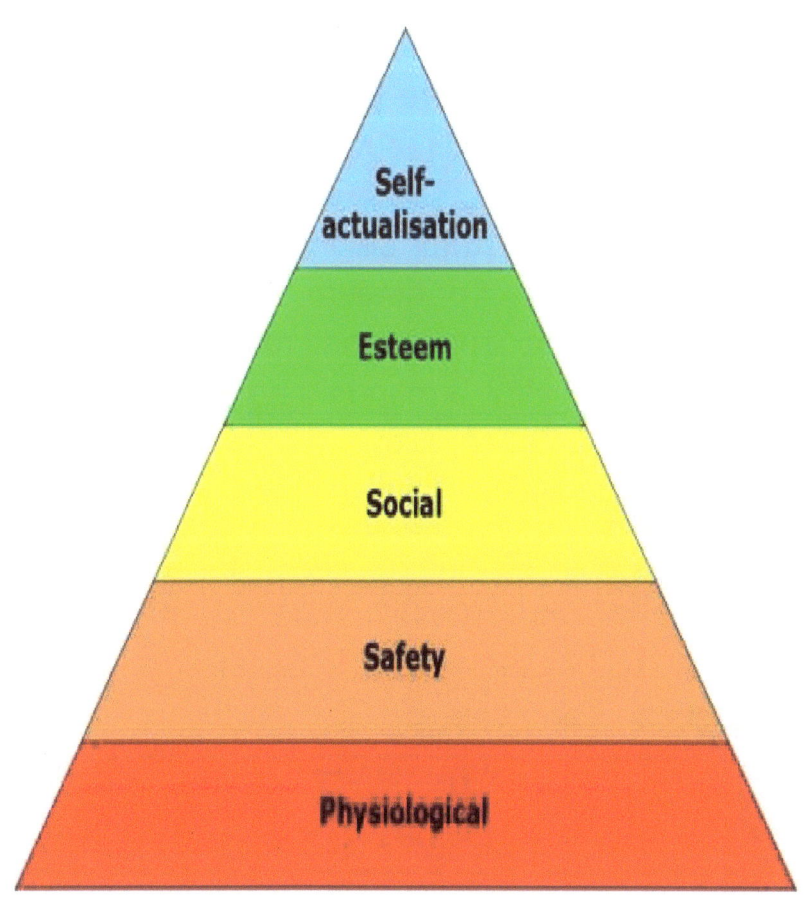

Maslow's Hierarchy of Needs pyramid

The physiological needs or in other words basic needs like food, water, and air are required for basic survival of a man. Once these are satisfied, an individual's safety needs take precedence like personal security, financial security and health security. Once these are taken care of, the third level of human needs such as love, intimacy, friendship take over. These are important as all humans have a need for belonging in the society. Then comes respect or esteem as all of us have a need to feel accepted and respected in the society. As a finality, a man has a need to achieve whatever his potential allows him to achieve or in other words to self actualize himself.

This hierarchy of needs helps the marketing professionals understand human nature and how to satisfy the same through marketing of various products and services.

Buyer's Decision Making Process

There are various factors and inputs that influence a buyer's decision towards buying any product or service.

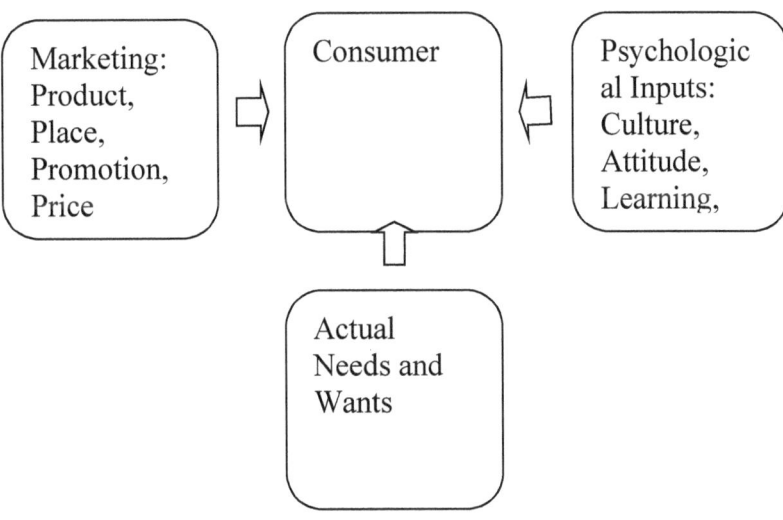

Other than his actual needs, a consumer gets influenced by his psychological inputs like the culture or background that he comes from, his attitude etc., all of which condition his perceptions towards a product or a service. Similarly marketing inputs such as the way the product is designed, how or through whom it is sold, its advertising and the price have a lot of influence in deciding what a consumer finally ends up buying.

Think of it this way, Tony may buy an iPhone because Amazon is giving a 40 % discount on its actual price. Rajesh may buy it because his work and lifestyle demand it since he has to use various data applications. Rossita may buy it because an iPhone is a status symbol and will put her into the elitist club. In her group of friends, what you possess defines who you are.

Key Concepts of Marketing

The Marketing Mix or the 4 P's of Marketing

Let us now delve into some of the basic tenets or constituents of marketing, commonly known as the 4P's of Marketing. These are:

Product

A product is an item or service that satisfies a consumer demand. It must be designed in a form and fashion that appeals to the consumer and satisfies his needs. If a product does not meet the customer needs, you can seldom make it a success. Let me tell you a story which I had read sometime back. There was a big meeting being held amongst the executives of a dog food company as their sales were not increasing despite all their marketing efforts. The gentleman responsible for Advertising got up and showed a really creative advertisement that they had been airing on national TV and claimed that it had won the Emmy Award. The gentleman responsible for Distribution got up and mentioned that they are now selling their dog food from all possible retail locations and also through Ecommerce websites so that people have complete ease of purchase and can buy food for their pets wherever, whenever. The executive responsible for Pricing mentioned that they have now reduced the price to make it really affordable so that people who feed regular home food to their dogs can also now shift to packaged dog food.

But there was one problem; the sales were still not increasing. So the whole team was debating and trying to find out where the problem lay. They seemed to be doing everything right.

A young executive then got up and meekly said "The problem is that the dogs don't like the food".

That tells us the importance of making sure that your product meets your customer's requirements. In this case the dog's!

The company then worked on improving the taste of their dog food and the sales started soaring thereafter.

Price

This is the amount the consumer has to pay for the product or the service. It is very important to keep the price of the product right so that the target customers can afford the product while at the same time the company is able to make a profit. Many products have a price elasticity which means the demand or sales of these products increases or decreases with the increase or decrease in price.

How many times have you liked a product but not bought it because it was expensive? "Many times", I am sure. Also, how many times would you have bought a product because it was on 'sale' or there was a discount being offered, even though you didn't really need it? Again, I am sure your answer would be, "many times". That's the power of pricing. It can swing your decision this way or that.

We are all aware about Mobile Phones. When the mobile services started in India in 1995, you had to pay Rs. 16 per minute for both incoming and outgoing calls and therefore the market remained limited. Then slowly the mobile companies started reducing the call charges and the market started expanding. Today there are no charges for incoming calls and the price per minute for an outgoing call is 1/50th of what it used to be when the service started. With the result, the market expanded rapidly and today almost everyone in India has a mobile phone, even if they find it difficult to make their both ends meet. This is the power of pricing.

You would have also noticed how Malls and Shops get crowded during the period when they are offering a 'Sale'. Price can be a big motivation as well as a big deterrent for people when they are considering to buy something.

Place

In marketing terms, 'place' refers to the channel or intermediary through which products and services move from the manufacturer to the consumer. In other words, how and from where a consumer can buy the product or service for example, through a retail shop, an Ecommerce website, door to door sales people or a catalogue. This has a profound effect on who will be your ultimate customers.

Would you buy an expensive 'Chanel' perfume from your neighborhood Grocer? My guess is not. You would instead prefer to buy it from a nice shop with a good ambience in a mall, airport or some other similar place or you may just order it from a reputed online store. Similarly, you wouldn't go to a mall to buy your day to day groceries, you would prefer to buy them from your neighborhood store instead. When it comes to books, most of the people prefer to buy books online these days, because of the convenience.

Making a product available for sales at a place where the consumer is most likely and comfortable to buy therefore is of paramount importance.

Xaomi

You would have recently observed that Xaomi (a Chinese Company) mobile phones became a rage amongst the youth and young professionals in China, India and other Asian countries. It is a phone with a friendly user interface and is especially suitable for high data users. Xaomi understood its market segment well and decided to launch and sell their phones in India only through India's largest Ecommerce website called Flipkart because they knew that most of their potential users would be young, upwardly mobile and internet savvy, who often do their purchases online.

Promotion

Promotion refers to how you communicate the benefits of the product or service to the consumers. This can be accomplished through a multitude of ways like personal selling through a sales person, direct mail, participation in trade fairs or advertising. There is often a stimuli required to push one into buying something. This could come by way of a salesman who is able to convince and persuade you or an incredible offer you receive in a direct mail or it could even be an advertisement in the TV or Newspapers which inspires you to buy the product.

Promotion or Marketing Communication or Advertising, as it is commonly known, is a scientific process based on human psychology and behavior. Any advertising or marketing campaign is designed to evoke any, some or all of the following outcomes in a potential buyer:

Attention

When a product is launched, its first goal is to **grab attention**. Companies spend huge amounts of money to grab consumer attention for their product. The method used to gain attention will depend on the product, market, target consumers, money available for spending etc. Options include sponsorship, hospitality events and large promotion campaigns through TV, Press, Outdoors and Internet. If the product is a gadget, a firm may decide to showcase it at a technology exhibition for example most of the new automobiles to be launched are showcased during the Autoshow which is visited by automobile enthusiasts, journalists and industry professionals. If the product is trendy and fashionable the firm may ask a celebrity who will appeal to the target market to endorse it.

Interest

Once you have secured people's attention and they are aware of the product, the next job is to **hold their interest**. This is done by promoting product features and clearly stating the benefit the product has to offer. The aim of the marketer at this stage is to provide the customer with information that will move them to the next stage of the process: Desire.

Desire

In the desire stage, your objective is to show your potential customers or prospects how your product or service can solve their problems. Explain the features of the product or service and the related benefits and demonstrate how the benefits fulfill the need. A common advertising process is the 'before and after' technique, such as when a cleaning product makes a soiled item look brand new. If done effectively, the potential customers or prospects should now have the desire to make a purchase. A unique selling point will help customers prefer your product over competitor's products. If your product is a trend setter, the latest 'must have' product, buzz marketing will help create a strong desire.

Action

Once a potential Customer has developed a desire for the product, the final step is to persuade the prospects to take immediate action. In a one-on-one sales process, this is the time to ask for the sale. In the advertising world, techniques involve creating sense of urgency by extending an offer for a limited time or including a bonus of special gift to those who act within a specific time frame. Without a specific call to action, the prospect may simply forget about your offer and move on. The task at this stage is to help the potential customer complete the purchase action by making it as simple as possible. For example, by offering a range of payment options and avenues like credit card, cheque, via high street shops and through the internet. If a company has been successful with its AIDA strategy then customers will purchase its products.

Some examples of promotion based on the above principle that you may recall are :

When Airtel (an Indian mobile phone operator) launched its cellular mobile services in India, they first put up huge Billboards with just their brand name on it to create an awareness and draw people's attention. This created a buzz and people started talking about Airtel and the concept of cellular mobile services.

As a next step Airtel launched its TV and Press campaigns telling people the details and benefits of using cellular mobile services. This created some interest in people's mind.

As a next step, Airtel identified its core target segment and positioned itself to cater to this segment. Their advertising thus spoke about business leaders and how they could become more effective and efficient using Airtel's mobile services. This helped create a desire amongst the potential target group.

Finally, Airtel offered some special schemes to attract people to sign up quickly such as discounted mobile phones or certain amount of free talk time etc. This helped potential customers make a decision and take the action to buy an Airtel connection.

The above would illustrate how the AIDA principle was effectively used.

A = Awareness
I = Interest
D = Desire
A = Action

Segmentation, Targeting and Positioning

Segmentation, Targeting and Positioning is an important three stage process in Marketing.

In the industry or sector that we want to serve, we first have to figure of what kind of customers exist, based on their needs or aspirations.

Let's take the case of a toothbrush. Some customers want a low price, some are keen on its design and features while others want durability. The customers, who want a low price, don't care about how long the product lasts. Whereas, the customers who are looking for design and features don't care about price. Similarly those looking for durability don't care about its features or how much the product costs. Now if you don't segment the market into blocks, and market the toothbrush in the same manner to everyone, you'll lose out on all the three blocks of customers - the customers looking for low cost would find the product not very desirable and the customers looking for design and features would find the toothbrush not up to the mark and the ones looking for durability may find it flimsy. However, proper segmentation of the market will allow you to first understand and then market the toothbrush as 'cheap' to one segment, 'feature rich' to another and "durable" to the third, thereby maximizing your sales.

Of course this was an oversimplification of the concept - in reality segments are often complex and there are many ways of their classification too. But I hope this simple example got the idea of segmentation and its importance across to you.

You can also extend the concept of segmentation to tea, and more specifically its temperature. You can serve hot tea and some people will enjoy it. You can serve ice tea and some people will enjoy it. However if you serve lukewarm tea, nobody enjoys it!

So one of the reasons to segment the market is because if you don't, you tend to go to the average value and this enables you to not meet anybody's needs.

Toyota Motor Company

Let's take a case study, of Toyota and Lexus. Incase, you didn't know both Toyota and Lexus are held by the same parent company.

When the regular Toyota was released it was not a high-end segment. It targeted a modest consumer base. In cars a very important factor is prestige. So whereas, the regular Toyota was hugely successful and made excellently engineered cars, they did not command the same prestige that would allow them to successfully enter the luxury car segment. So Toyota Motor Company created the high-end luxury segment brand Lexus. All the high-end luxury vehicles created by Toyota are sold under the brand name Lexus. While this allows the more modestly earning customers - who value a modest price -to purchase the regular Toyota series, it also allows the high end customers who value prestige over price to be satisfied by purchasing a vehicle which is not associated with the modestly priced regular Toyota.

If we were to formally define Market Segmentation, "It is the process of dividing up the market into distinct subsets, where any subset could conceivably be selected and then you pick one of those market segments to be your target. And you reach or you deliver to that customer segment, that market segment, with a distinct marketing mix."

What this means in context of the **marketing mix** i.e. the four P's - product, place, promotion and price is that when we are looking at different segments, they may want different products. It may make sense to advertise them differently. It may make sense to price differently and also be sold through different channels. So that's how segmentation becomes useful.

Targeting

After segmenting the market based on different groups and classes, you will need to choose your targets. No one strategy will suit all consumer groups, so being able to develop specific strategies for your target markets is very important.

There are three general strategies for selecting your target markets:

Undifferentiated Targeting: This approach views the market as a single group with no individual segments, therefore using a single marketing strategy. This strategy may be useful for a business or product which is a commodity with little or no competition where you may not need to tailor strategies for different customer preferences.

For example Tata Salt markets its salt to all classes of customers since it is an essential commodity.

Concentrated Targeting: This approach focuses on selecting a particular market segment and then focusing all marketing efforts on this segment. One should develop an in-depth understanding of the needs and wants of the selected market segment and then concentrate all strategies and efforts to serve them. Small companies with a single or a limited range of products often benefit from this strategy as focusing on one segment enables them to compete effectively against larger companies with a diverse range of products.

As an example, Virtu markets its mobile phones to a very small niche of ultra rich socialites who are very design and image conscious.

Multi-Segment Targeting: This segmentation approach is used if you need to focus on two or more well defined market segments and want to develop different strategies for them. Multi segment targeting is becoming quite prevalent these days as customers are becoming very individualistic in their tastes and choices. It offers many benefits but can be costly as it involves greater resources in terms of increased market research and increased promotional/advertising initiatives.

Again Nokia's 'Asha' range of feature phones is targeted to first time users who are looking at value for money in India – it is primarily sold in the rural areas. Its 'N Series' was targeted at young music lovers. The 'Lumia' range of smart phones is for the youth who are heavy data users and like to download a lot of Mobile Apps. Virtu is for the ultra rich segment.

Prior to selecting a particular targeting strategy, one needs to do a full analysis including cost benefit to determine that the segment can give enough business at the right price so that the business can be profitable because ultimately the object of doing business is to earn a profit.

Positioning

Positioning is defined as the act of designing a product and its communication in a manner so as to occupy a distinctive position in the minds of the consumer. A strong positioning for a product or a service automatically draws a consumer towards it.

If you look at the Social Networking arena:

Facebook is positioned as a strong medium for social interaction between friends and family. Linkedin is positioned for working professionals and Snapchat for quick instant communication between teenagers.

If you want to connect with people professionally, you would automatically think of Linkedin. Similarly if you are a teenager wanting to stay in touch with your boyfriend or girlfriend then the first thing that comes to your mind would perhaps be Snapchat.

Product positioning is an important element of a marketing plan. Product positioning is the process marketers use to determine how to best communicate their products' attributes to their target customers based on customer needs, competitive pressures, available communication channels and carefully crafted key messages. It determines how the product is *placed* in the market, and how is it perceived by its target segment. Effective product positioning ensures that marketing messages resonate with target consumers and compel them to take action.

When considering the positioning of a product in the market the following questions will and should come to our mind:

- What place does a product occupy in the market?

- How does a particular product stack up against its competition in the market?

- What are the consumer's attitudes and perceptions towards the product in question?

Given this view, the product (brand) positioning is assessed by measuring the target market segment's perceptions of and preferences for the product in relation to its competitors.

The importance of Positioning can best be understood by taking the following brief case studies.

Tata Nano

The Nano is a car which was launched by TATA Motors in India a few years back with an advertised ex-showroom price of Rs. 100,000 equivalent to approximately $1,800 at current exchange rates. As such it was the cheapest car ever produced.

It was also marketed as being the cheapest car in the Indian market. 'Cheapest' was what Tata Motors believed would attract customers towards it - a man who could afford only a motor bike could now own a car. Thus, Tata Motors expected that the car would sell to the masses in massive quantities. However, this was not to be so, though sales initially began at a high point, they soon fizzled out and as of last year I believe only 200 Nano cars were sold across India.

The numbers perplexed Tata Dealerships across the nation. Why wasn't the Nano a big hit? Why did it not sell as much as it was expected to prior to its release? The answer is simple; because it was the cheapest car of the lot. Ratan Tata, the Chairman of the company made a public statement after about three years of its release, on why the car did not sell as much as any other car. He said, "The car was perfect, however the marketing was not." When someone wants to buy a car, besides reasons of it being comfortable or convenient, here in India, it is also to lift their social status. You want a car, to show others how you have risen in society. And that's where Nano failed to satisfy its customers. It ran smooth on the road, but as soon as someone saw it from the outside, they were reminded that it was the cheapest car. Therefore people saved up and bought other cars over the Nano, which were more expensive, but gave them the respect and public imagery which they wanted.

That's where marketing plays an important role. Your product could be the best of the lot; but if that's not conveyed to the public, you wouldn't get many customers.

Soaps

If you look at various soaps available in the market, you may feel that a soap is an inconsequential product and therefore does not merit too much deliberation. However, on a deeper scrutiny each of the soap brands is very carefully positioned in order to serve the desires and aspirations of its target segment. 'Lux' is for the beauty conscious segment who aspire to look like celebrities. Its tagline therefore is "Soap for the film stars'. 'Liril' on the other hand is positioned as a soap that brings about freshness and therefore all its advertising is built around the concept of freshness. 'Lifebuoy' is positioned as a health soap which helps fight bacteria and was primarily used for washing hands although they have been trying to change that position so that they can broadbase their target segment. Similarly 'Cetaphil' is positioned as a cleanser with its flagship product called 'Daily Facial Cleanser'. Each of us, based on our needs, wants and aspirations would pick up a soap that is most suited to us based on the positioning that soap has established in our mind.

Google

How many of you have seen the advertisement of Google- 'Dear Sophie'? If not, I will strongly recommend you to watch it. The video is about one and a half minutes long. The main objective of the Advertisement is to show to the viewers, how much you can do via Google. And Google has been able to spread their message very beautifully. It's about a father who saves the milestone moments of his daughter's life right from the day she was born, her brother's birth, ballet lessons, a face pack; in the form of pictures, recordings and videos. At the end he says "You're growing up so fast. I can't wait to share these with you someday. Love, Dad" This video has gotten almost 10 million views on YouTube.

The effectiveness and subtlety with which they have communicated the strength of Google's services is amazing.

In some way this video conveys the positioning of Google which is seen as an all encompassing service by many of us.

Another good example of how a brand has positioned itself and done effective promotion based on its positioning is:

BlendTec

An example of simple but effective positioning and its promotion was done by a man named Tom Dickson. He founded a company named BlendTec, which manufactures Blenders.

Because of lack of resources he wasn't able to advertise for his blenders in conventional media like Newspapers, Magazines or Television. However, he was confident of the strength of his product. So what he did was, that he started uploading his product videos on YouTube. In each video, he would put an electrical gadget such as an iPhone, iPad, etc. in his Blender and switch it on to show it blend into dust. He would then finally open the Blender to demonstrate that there was nothing left but powder.

The job was done for him. People got the message about the strength and ruggedness of his product. The videos went viral and the viewership of his videos has gone up to 20 million, and the company is growing very rapidly. Infact, the sales of BlendTec have increased by upto 700 percent after the release of the first 'Will it blend?' video. 'Will it Blend' is a much awaited event now as each time a new iPhone comes out, Tom Dickson makes it a public event by putting the newly released iPhone into the Blender and converting it into dust.

So by spending virtually no money, Dickson was able to showcase his Blenders and bring them to the forefront of the market, giving stiff competition to companies such as Whirlpool, Philips and LG.

Brand

What is a Brand? Here's what I have learnt: A brand denotes the personality of a product. A brand is the set of expectations, memories, stories and relationships that, taken together, account for a consumer's decision to choose one product or service over another. If the consumer (be it a business, a buyer, a voter or a donor) doesn't pay a premium, make a selection or spread the word, then no brand value exists for that consumer.

The exercise and actions required for establishing the brand are called branding and may include the following:

Define your Brand Personality. First thing to do when you want to create a brand is to define and clearly lay out the brand personality or attributes you would like it to have.

Create a logo. Put it everywhere but most importantly in places that synchronize with your brand values.

Write down your brand messaging. What are the key messages you want to communicate about your brand? Everyone and especially your target segment should be aware of your brand attributes.

Integrate your brand into your business operations. Branding extends to every aspect of your business - advertising, letterheads, how you answer your phones, what you or your salespeople wear on sales calls, your e-mail signature - everything.

Create a 'tone' for your company that reflects your brand. This should reflect in all written and oral communication and also incorporated in the visual imagery in all media. Is your brand friendly? Be conversational. Be formal or informal based on your brand attributes.

Develop a tagline. Write a memorable, meaningful and concise statement that captures the essence of your brand. Remember Mercedes Benz's 'Engineered like no other Car' or BMW's

'The Ultimate Driving Machine'. Google's 'Don't be Evil' or Nike's 'Just Do it'.

Establish Brand Guidelines. Use the same color scheme, logo placement, look and feel throughout. You don't have to be fancy, you must however be consistent.

Be true to your brand. Deliver on your brand promise. You must provide to your consumers what you have got them to expect.

Be consistent. Just like your personal credibility, it takes a long time for the brand to get established and during this period you have to be consistent with all the above points.

These days, brands understand that being a brand is not enough, rather they must be "the brand of choice". Further, brands understand that in order to really be the brand of choice, you have to understand what happens when a consumer becomes a shopper. What this means is to understand the decision making process from a shopper's point-of-view. We need to understand that consumers make impulse purchase decisions. They buy on habit, intuition, by making decisions based on what they see and what they don't see. The brand has to be relevant to the shopper's life in order to make sense to the shopper. And this shopper process, is a multi-channeled process.

In order to be able to implement this, we need to understand the two most useful principles of marketing or the key concepts of marketing as they are called - Customer Centricity and Product Centricity.

.

Key Approaches to Marketing

Before taking up the "Key Concepts of Marketing" in depth, I am sure you are already familiar with the 4P's of marketing which we covered in one of the earlier chapters. That will allow you to better understand the following concepts.

Customer Centricity

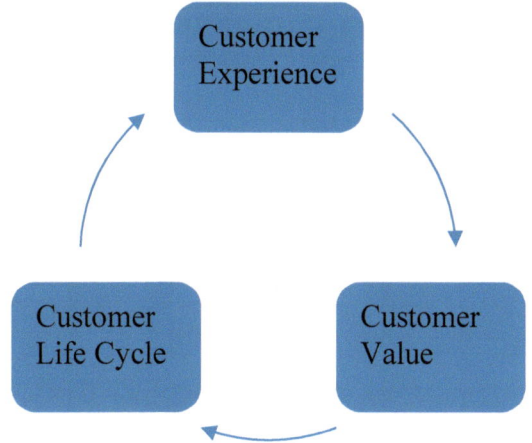

The idea of focusing on maximizing the long-term financial value of certain kinds of customers, is what customer centricity is all about.

The first corner stone of Consumer Centricity is that, whatever cons the customers perceive, is what affects their subsequent actions and behavior.

Second, and this is what's interesting, is that what they perceive is not necessarily what's true. Why is that? Well, the process of perception is constructive. And this process is inherently biased. It contains the process of perception that comes in several different stages. The first two stages are, the stages of attention and exposure. Before you can form any kind of perception, you need to be exposed to the stimuli. And you need to pay attention to that stimuli. Pay attention to what's salient to you.

It's important for you, as a seller, to realize that some customers are more valuable than others. And these "valuable" customers are the ones on whom you'll try the various methods of increasing profit. This can be done by a few very strategic and common methods- Cross-selling, Up-selling, Frequency and Margins.

When we go to McDonalds and order a Burger, the crew member taking our order, very occasionally asks us, "Would you like fries with that?" This is an example of cross selling. **Cross-selling** is the idea of getting customers to buy more than just the particular product that they're interested in. Getting people to buy other products. They can either be from the same product category like amazon.com recommending other books to you, or other product categories.

Next to cross-selling would be up-selling.

The classic fast food example there would be: "Do you want to super size it?" So that's how you try to get people to buy a higher margin version of the same item. **Up-selling**, again is very common not just in fast food but in financial services and many other industries. You want to get people who are going to buy something, to buy a 'better' or 'larger' something.

Now we move onto frequency.

The classic fast-food example of frequency would be offering a loyalty card. Get 10 points for every Burger you buy and when you collect 100 points you get a free Burger. Frequency aims at getting customers not only to buy something but to buy that something again and again, more frequently!

And the fourth one, which companies don't like to talk about, what they like to do or at least wish they could do, would be through selectively increasing margins.

Maybe not just up-selling but maybe we can get people to pay more money for the same product or service. A lot of companies are very hesitant to do that. They don't want to mess around, charging different prices for the same product or service to different people. However, using this method of changing the **Margin**, makes lots of sense. For instance, Apple charges a lower rate for University students than for regular buyers.

Product Centricity

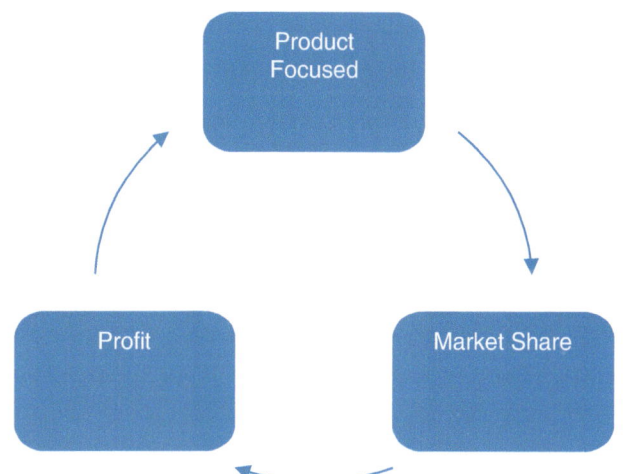

Why would one want to set up a business? What is the primary objective of a company? Well, the answer seems obvious, doesn't it? To make a profit, and then maximize that profit over a period of time. And broadly speaking, for the better part of the past century, all companies have used the same general strategy to achieve that goal. That strategy can be termed "Product Centricity."

During a recent weekend break, my parents visited a plants nursery. Seeing loads of orange, apple and guava plants, they decided to buy something for our backyard. My mother wanted an orange plant, which would soon grow into a tree. When she asked the gardener to show her the plants, he showed her three different plants at three different stages of growth. The smallest one was about three feet tall, and was hundred rupees. The next one was about four feet tall, and the one after that about five feet tall, with price tags of a thousand rupees and of two thousand rupees respectively.

The tree worth two thousand rupees, was the only one which had fruits hanging from it. However, on having a further conversation with the gardener my mother learnt that the fruits will fall of in another four to five days, since winter had just started, and orange trees shed their fruits during the season. During further conversation it came out that all the three types of plants would start yielding fruit at about the same time. So, there was no real differentiator in the three plants from a usability or productivity point of view. However, the plant with oranges hanging from it looked appealing and attracted my mother's attention, and she bought the five feet plant for rupees two thousand. In fact, the five feet plant, was being bought by most of the people who were wanting to buy an orange plant!

This is an example of product centricity. How an object of the same value, can be sold at different prices, and thus earning a greater profit.

Let's consider a scenario; you have a product - that is something which customers want / need. Further, customers have more than a hundred options of companies to buy that product from. Thus, to make sure that customers come to you and do not go to your competition, you should keep innovating on that product, you should try to reduce its cost and you should really focus and add some differentiating features in the product. Your business objective in a product-focused market is to sell as much as you can, and profitably.

What's the best way to get the customer to buy from your store rather than from the competition?

The best way to do it is to look at what that customer wants, and deliver a product that meets the needs of that customer in the best possible manner.

Google's entire strategy and approach is Product Centric. They keep improving their 'search engine' and 'user experience' with the result that users prefer them over any other search engine and they have over a 70% market share in 'search'.

Think about blood donation. The American Red Cross used marketing principles to get an increase in blood donations. What is the "product" for the American Red Cross when they want more blood? It's not blood, is it? Because that's not what they are selling; that's what they are getting in return. Blood, is actually the price. It's what the customer puts into the exchange. Then what is the product? What the American Red Cross did was try to figure out ways to get people to be more willing to donate more blood. They tried to make people 'feel good' about themselves for donating blood. You're going to help save lives. This method worked for some people. For some people, that wasn't enough. They needed a little sticker that said, "Yes, I gave blood today and I saved lives". For other people, the orange juice and the cookies were enough. So American Red Cross kept improving and offering different Products - feel good factor, badges, recognition, juice and cookies to attract different client types who had to pay the price i.e., their 'blood' to get one of these.

Product based marketing is affected by some basic tenants, which are listed as follows:

1. **Technological advances** and the speed with which new technologies are created and copied.

2. **Globalization** and the geographic advantages that have been lost as a result.

3. **Deregulation** and the way it has shaken up traditionally stable industries.

4. **The rising power of the consumer** and their newfound ability to get what they want, whenever they want, from whomever they want.

Consumers are smarter than ever before. The market is more saturated than ever before, more competitive than ever before, and changing more quickly than ever before. It is the perfect storm, and it explains why today's consumers are so demanding – the simple reason is that because they can afford to be demanding.

Marketing Strategy

Assuming that you have a product or a service that is ready to be sold, then what should be your next step.

You should start by making a proper plan on what to do, when to do and how to do it. Below is an illustrative method on how to market a product.

These are some of the steps that can be used.

Making a Marketing Strategy

Every marketing strategy should answer a basic question- Why will customers want to buy your product or service rather than that of your competition?

Marketing strategies happen at various different levels. For larger companies, a strategy is created at the corporate level, the SBU or the strategic business unit level, and the product level.

In smaller companies, the process may not be followed methodically but most entrepreneurs and business people would unknowingly think through and discuss the same issues within the same group of employees.

Either way, while doing this, you need to keep two things in mind:

a) Your product's compétitive advantage.
b) The Customer's needs, desires and expectations should be fulfilled.

Firstly, estimate the product's sales and profits in the first few years of being in the market.

Secondly, establish the planned price, name, quantity, material, design, features, etc.

Lastly, project the product's long run sales and profits. After you are done coming up with a strategy, it's important to define a Marketing Process.

The Marketing Process

When you are starting a new company or planning to launch a new product or approach a new market, it is a good practice to have a professional approach to Marketing and hence analyze marketing opportunities, identify target customers, understand their needs, and know your competition. Briefly speaking, the marketing process involves the following :

Develop a marketing strategy (as explained earlier). Brainstorm new product ideas, define your brand, its competitive edge, etc.

Create a marketing plan. Decide how you'll position, price and promote a product, which distribution channels you'll use and so forth.

Act on your marketing strategy/ plan. Be prepared for highs and lows.

Evaluate the effectiveness of your marketing strategy and plan, and adjust them accordingly.

Acknowledgements

After having gone through an internship at an advertising company 'Metal' and doing a course in Marketing from Coursera, when I decided to put my pen to paper and share my interest, learning and understanding of Marketing with my fellow school children, it appeared to be a daunting task; little did I realize that the subject of marketing had already somewhat prepared me to accomplish this task. My internship at 'Metal' kindled my interest in Marketing and hence I would like to thank Mr. Probir Dutt for accepting me as an intern. I would also like to thank my various colleagues at Metal whom I kept pestering with my silly questions. My thanks to Coursera and the faculty there. I initially found the course daunting but soon adapted well to their rhythm. I would also like to thank the man who named me and was perhaps one of India's best known professionals Mr. Prakash Tandon (first Indian Chairman of Hindustan Levers Limited) who although is no more now, left an indelible impression on me in my formative years to stretch myself and accomplish something. My brother Siddharth Mehta was a big source of encouragement and also a sounding board who very ably assisted me in writing this book. And finally I would like to thank my mother Sona for reminding me every day (sometime multiple times in a day!) that the Book was still pending, putting morning alarms and then unsuccessfully trying to wake me up. Without her, the Book would not have seen the light of the day.

I must acknowledge that I have referred liberally to Google and other papers, books and articles while compiling this book and hence you may see some tones of the same in this book.

I would also like to thank my School, our Principal and my Teachers for giving me an environment and inculcating in me a spirit to create and share knowledge.

Finally, please consider this book as a novice's attempt to explain marketing to school kids and therefore any mistakes or shortcomings are solely mine and may please be overlooked

www.ingramcontent.com/pod-product-compliance
Lightning Source LLC
Chambersburg PA
CBHW040907180526
45159CB00010BA/2960